The
Connell Short Guide
to
Sebastian Faulks's

———————————

Birdsong

———————————

by
David Isaacs

Contents

Introduction

People love *Birdsong*. To date, it has sold more than three million copies. Countless stage adaptations have been made; in 2012 it was turned into a two-part BBC series starring Eddie Redmayne and Clémence Poésy; a Hollywood film, starring Nicholas Hoult, is currently in production. It scores highly in lists of the nation's favourite books. (It came 13th in the BBC's Big Read in 2003, for example.) And it has barely had a bad word written about it; some critics even think it only just stops short of perfection. "So powerful is this recreated past," wrote Sue Gee in The Times, "that you long to call *Birdsong* perfect." "*Birdsong* is not a perfect novel," Simon Schama wrote in the New Yorker, "just a great one."

But its subject matter is tough. The First World War was a catastrophe beyond the scale of anything that Europe had seen before: 37 million casualties, 16 million deaths, and historians still can't agree on why it was fought, why so many men were sent to their deaths in such abysmal conditions. Words like "unimaginable" and "unspeakable" are commonly used to describe this war – as if the only adequate way to speak of its horror is to acknowledge the lack of an adequate way to speak of it – and yet, in *Birdsong*, Sebastian Faulks imagined it, spoke of it, and did so in a way that millions of people have taken to their hearts.

A summary of the plot

Birdsong has seven main parts, spanning three different time periods. In Part One, set in 1910, Stephen Wraysford, a hot-blooded and enigmatic young Englishman, is on a research trip to France, staying with the rich Azaire family in the town of Amiens. René Azaire is a snobbish factory owner involved in the textile industry and Stephen has been sent to him to learn about the French manufacturing process. He falls in love with Azaire's beautiful young wife, Isabelle and they run away together; Isabelle, guilt-ridden and secretly pregnant, returns to Amiens, and Stephen, devastated by her desertion, ends up staying in France.

Part Two jumps to 1916: a team of men is digging a tunnel underneath no man's land during the First World War. Faulks introduces us to a hardly known aspect of the combat, the war that was fought underground in narrow, airless tunnels. We follow one of the tunnelers, Jack Firebrace. Jack is castigated by an officer for falling asleep on duty – and soon we learn that the officer is Stephen. We meet Stephen's friend Michael Weir, and his immediate superior, Captain Gray. The section ends with a harrowing description of the Battle of the Somme.

In Part Three we are suddenly in 1978, following a businesswoman called Elizabeth Benson. She turns out to be Stephen's granddaughter, but knows very little about him. After reading a newspaper article commemorating the war, and discovering Stephen's wartime diaries in her mother's attic, she resolves to find out more.

In Part Four we're back in the war, in 1917. Stephen, by chance, sees Isabelle's sister Jeanne in a bar, and asks her how Isabelle is. Jeanne takes Stephen to her. She is having an affair with a German soldier; she and Stephen say goodbye and will not see each other again. Later, we learn that Stephen and Jeanne married after the war.

In Part Five, we are back with Elizabeth, who is now interviewing the few survivors of the war she can find who knew Stephen – including Captain Gray, now an old man.

Part Six takes us back to 1918 and culminates with Stephen and Jack Firebrace trapped underground for days after a German attack on the tunnels. The perspective shifts to that of a Jewish German soldier named Levi, who rescues Stephen, though Jack has died. When Stephen emerges from underground, the war is over; he and Levi embrace, and become friends.

In Part Seven Elizabeth learns that Isabelle was her grandmother, not Jeanne as she had previously thought. In the final chapter, she gives birth to a boy, whom she names after Jack Firebrace's dead son, John.

War

In the introduction to the novel's tenth anniversary edition, Faulks writes: "The major theme... was this: how far can you go? What are the limits of humanity?" For Faulks, the war was, above all, extreme; its scale and brutality marked something new. *Birdsong* explores what happens to a human being, and his or her sense of self, when pushed to such extremity; at what point, it asks, do you stop being human?

The centerpiece is an unflinching reimagining of the Battle of the Somme. This was when the war pushed hardest at the limits of human experience, when it reached new extremes. A minor character, Arthur Shaw, feels this as he watches it unfold:

> *Shaw stood with his mouth open. He was unmoved by violence, hardened to the mutilation he had seen and inflicted, but what he was watching here was something of a different order. (229)*

So extreme is it, in fact, that the division's priest, Horrocks, "pulled the silver cross from his chest and hurled it from him. His old reflex still persisting, he fell to his knees, but he did not pray" (230). God is dead; religion, belief – the systems that give meaning to human life, that sustain an individual's sense of self – are here reduced to a "persisting reflex". "Nothing was divine any more,"

Stephen thinks, "everything was profane" (230).

Stephen is frightened, as he prepares to go over the top, not by what might happen to his body – his "particles of flesh" (219) – but by what might happen to his sense of self:

> *He felt no fear for his blood and muscle and bone, but the size of what had begun, the number of them now beneath the terrible crashing of the sky was starting to pull at the mooring of his self-control. (219)*

"Self-control" here refers to the structures people erect to hold their ideas of themselves in place. He is frightened that at a point of such extremity - he thinks: "This was the worst; nothing had been like this" (219) - those structures will collapse. When we next see him, a year later, all his character – everything that made him 'Stephen' rather than simply "blood and muscle and bone" – seems to have drained from him:

> *His eyes had always been dark, but now they seemed shrunk. There was no light in them. His voice, which had once reverberated with meanings and nuances, with temper and emotions held in check, was now alternately toneless or barking. He seemed a man removed to some new existence where he was dug in and fortified by his lack of natural feeling or response. (334)*

This is the cost of war, the limit of humanity. The slaughter is seen through Stephen's eyes with what John Mullan calls "numbed precision".

Faulks is not an historian, but the novel does, subtly, suggest how such a disaster might have been allowed to happen. The first 100 or so pages, which tell Stephen and Isabelle's story, contain a couple of clues. On the surface, this love story seems to have little in it that might indicate any causes of the First World War. But there is a subplot whose relevance to the novel is, at first glance, easy to miss.

The men who work in Azaire's factory are on strike; their working conditions are poor, their wages low, and they are in danger of losing their jobs to new machines that can do the work better and faster. Azaire has strikingly little compassion for them. "What these strikers need," he says,

> *"is for someone to call their bluff. I'm not prepared to see my business stagnate because of the gross demands of a few idle men. Some owner has to have the strength to stand up to them and sack the whole lot." (13)*

Later, when an elected representative tries to negotiate with him, Stephen is shocked by how little Azaire even pretends to care:

> *Stephen was surprised by the simplicity of Azaire's*

assault. He made no pretense that the work force had anything to gain from the new arrangements or that they would make up in some other way for what they were clearly being asked to forgo. (21)

(Note, here, Faulks's use of the word "assault", the language of battle: a foreshadowing of things to come.) And when he learns that Isabelle has been secretly giving food to strikers' families, Azaire's response – a mixture of horror and incomprehension; he brands her actions "selfish" (94) – is telling. The right response to these workers' suffering, the novel suggests, is Isabelle's: compassion and charity. The ruling class, however, of which Azaire is here a representative, is just not capable of seeing members of the working class as human beings worthy of compassion.

In *Birdsong*'s second section, on the eve of the Battle of the Somme, Azaire is long forgotten. But he has a counterpart, another member of the ruling class: Colonel Barclay. Barclay, a minor character who appears in only a few pages, is significant. He is more interested in what's for dinner than the fate of his men: when Stephen and his superior, Captain Gray, suggest that the Somme offensive might not be such a good idea, Barclay responds dismissively – "I've never come across two such faint-hearts" (211) – before adding: "Now let's go and have lunch." Even in his rallying speech to the soldiers before the push, he measures their imagined success in gastronomical terms; at its climax he yells (referring to a part of France under German occupation): "I believe we shall take dinner in Bapaume"(216). We know Barclay's type; we've met someone like him before.

In 1916 the British Army, barring the officer class, was drawn almost entirely from the working classes. Back in England, workers – who, like those in Azaire's factory, were widely on strike – were sold the idea of fighting the war as a great adventure. (It would be "over by Christmas" they were told in 1914.) In his book *World War One: A Short History*, the historian Norman Stone describes how "British volunteers, in millions, had abandoned the boredom of life in industrial towns for the supposed glamour of a soldier's existence". The soldiers were, in other words, sold a lie and nearly a million working-class men were sent without hesitation to their deaths. Though it is never directly addressed in the novel, Faulks allows us to trace a line from Azaire's indifference to his workers' suffering to Barclay's gung-ho dismissal of Stephen and Gray's anxieties, and draw our own conclusions: Barclay, and the officer class he represents, so Faulks is implying, saw the lives of the working classes as dispensable.*

An army is an institution, and in institutions, as Stephen thinks of the orphanage in which he grew up, people are "reduced to numbers, to ranks of nameless people who were not valued in the eyes

A still taken from the 1916 propaganda film The Battle of the Somme, *made before the actual battle to depict trench warfare. It played to packed cinemas to boost morale*

of another individual" (104). (Once again, the relevance of this idea to the war sections of the novel is signaled by the military language: in this case, the word ranks.) Faulks captures the extent to which the soldiers were "reduced... to ranks of nameless people" and denied their individuality in his memorable descriptions, such as this one, of

* This is the subject of many of Siegfried Sassoon's poems, such as this deceptively jolly rhyme, 'The General':

'GOOD-MORNING; good-morning!' the General said
When we met him last week on our way to the line.
Now the soldiers he smiled at are most of 'em dead,
And we're cursing his staff for incompetent swine.
'He's a cheery old card,' grunted Harry to Jack
As they slogged up to Arras with rifle and pack.

. . . .

But he did for them both by his plan of attack.

the Somme:

> *Stephen... could see a long, wavering line of khaki,*
> *primitive dolls progressing in tense, deliberate steps,*
> *going down with a silent flap of arms, replaced, falling,*
> *continuing as though walking into a gale. (226)*

The men are all the same: "primitive dolls" – unfeeling puppets – who are easily replaceable. Their efforts are futile ("walking into a gale") and their death makes no noise ("with a silent flap of arms"). It is as if they are nothing more than toy soldiers: Jack Firebrace thinks: "They were men who could each have had a history but, in the shadow of what awaited them, were interchangeable" (144). If, instead of their attitude of indifference to individual working-class lives, an attitude which Barclay represents, the officers had been able to see each soldier as an individual human being with his own history – which is what the novel seeks to do – the carnage would never have been allowed to happen.

Barclay is also representative of something else: the old world. Or, to be more exact: the old world's ignorance of a new, emerging world. Norman Stone describes the clash of old and new that was such a significant part of this war:

> In four years, the world went from 1870 to 1940.
> In 1914, cavalry cantered off to stirring music, the

Austrian Prince Clary-Aldringen wore the uniform he had put on for a gala at Buckingham Palace, and early illustrations of the war show clumps of infantry charging with bayonets, as shrapnel explodes overhead. It is 1870. Fortresses were readied for prolonged sieges, medical services were still quite primitive, and severely wounded men were likely to die. By 1918, matters had become very different, and French generals had already devised a new method of warfare, in which tanks, infantry and aircraft collaborated, in the manner of the German Blitzkrieg ('lightning war') of 1940. Cavalry regiments became museum-pieces, and fortresses, relics... Medicine made greater progress in these four years than at any time before or after: by 1918, only 1 per cent of wounded men died.

He concludes: "No war has ever begun with such a fundamental misunderstanding of its nature." This misunderstanding, for Faulks, is another factor that made the Somme possible. This was not a war that could be fought in the old way; this was a war of machines. Barclay just doesn't see it.

The technological advances were many but most iconic is the early use of machine guns. Stephen understands what Barclay doesn't:

At first he thought the war could be fought and

concluded swiftly in a traditional way. Then he
watched the machine gunners pouring bullets into
the lines of advancing German infantry as though
there was no longer any value accorded to a mere
human life... he watched the men harden to the
mechanical slaughter. (162)

The key phrase here is 'mechanical slaughter'; with the use of machine guns, death became impersonal.

Once again, this is foreshadowed in the first section, in which technological advances mean workers losing jobs. "They complain they are losing their jobs because we have introduced machinery," moans Azaire, "but if we cannot compete with our competitors in Spain and England then we have no hope" (6). Later, he refers happily to a "greater use of machinery and a consequent loss of jobs" (20). Replace the word "jobs" with "lives" and you have the idea.

In *Birdsong* even the air is metal: "The air overhead was solid metal" (217); "It was though he had become detached, in a dream, from the metal air through which his flesh was walking" (226); "A whistle blew, and clumsily the men began to clamber up the ladders, weighed down by their heavy packs, into the metal air" (353). Faulks is referring poetically to the sheer number of bullets being fired at speed, but it is a fitting metaphor for the new technological basis of warfare. And in this metal air, the army's adherence to tradition looks absurd. Soldiers were commanded to walk slowly across no man's land because that was a traditional British tactic. But there were no machine guns in previous wars and in this one the soldiers were commanded, in effect, to climb into a "mechanised abattoir" (353) and do as little as they could to avoid being killed. And where's Colonel Barclay? Doggedly sticking to the old ways, riding on an "indolently snorting horse" like a "character from comic opera" (215) and "carrying a sword" (226). His bravery is immense – and it must be remembered that the officers in this war were brave, that they willingly gave their own lives to the cause – but the absurd picture Faulks paints, of the old world ignoring the new, is shattering.

One outcome of the newness of this war was that there was no language with which to talk about it. "I have been under fire," Stephen thinks at one point. "Under fire. The words came back. How thin and inadequate the phrase was" (362). The old language is not enough and the soldiers are doomed to not being able to communicate their experiences. "No one in England knows what this is like," Stephen thinks of life in the trenches. "If they could see the way these men live they would not believe their eyes" (150). But they couldn't see and, according to the poet Siegfried Sassoon – who served on the Western Front – many of them didn't want to: in 1917 he wrote a letter to The Times condemning

the callous complacency with which the majority

of those at home regard the continuance of agonies which they do not share, and which they have not sufficient imagination to realise.

The basis of Sassoon's anger is illustrated in one of the novel's most painful scenes, which takes place not on the battlefield, but in the cosy Warwickshire home of Stephen's best friend in the trenches, Captain Michael Weir. After the Somme, Weir goes on leave and surprises his parents by arriving unannounced on their doorstep. Faulks sets up the scene perfectly: we expect an overwhelmed mother flinging her arms round her son – unexpectedly back from the war, alive, well – and a father looking on with pride. But this is not what happens. They hardly acknowledge his arrival. "You'd better come on in then," Weir's father says by way of a greeting. "Why didn't you tell us you were coming?" (287). "You look a bit thin, Michael", his mother says, without even a hello, "What have they been feeding you on over in France?" (288). She clearly doesn't have much imagination if she thinks a poor diet is the extent of her son's suffering.

The closest Weir's father gets to mentioning the war is when he asks: "I expect you'd like a bit of company after all... after, you know." "France?" Weir asks. "Exactly," his father replies (289). But this is not exact at all, it is highly indirect. Weir himself gets closest to mentioning it: "It's been terrible... I've got to tell you, it's been –." But then: "I mean, you can't imagine." And, clearly, as Sassoon would have understood, Weir's father has no interest in imagining: "Everyone's doing their bit, you know," he says (289).

But it's not just impossible to communicate to people back home: the soldiers can't even explain it to themselves. As the psychologist William Rivers thinks in Pat Barker's World War One novel, *Regeneration*: "They'd been trained to identify emotional repression as the essence of manliness." As a result, they have no way of addressing their extreme experiences. Jack Firebrace understands this when he and his mates have a night off and go out on the town:

> *None of these men would admit that what they saw and what they did were beyond the boundaries of human behavior. You would not believe, Jack thought, that the fellow with his cap pushed back, joking with his friend at the window of the butcher's shop, had seen his other mate dying in a shellhole, gas frothing in his lungs. No one told; and Jack too joined the unspoken conspiracy that all was well, that no natural order had been violated. (141)*

Weir says: "I've got to tell you", but can't; Jack thinks: "No one told." The outcome of no-one telling is that everyone forgets. Stephen acknowledges this in his diary, which ends with these words:

No child or future generation will ever know what this was like. They will never understand.

When it is over we will go quietly among the living and we will not tell them.

We will talk and sleep and go about our business like human beings.

We will seal what we have seen in the silence of our hearts and no words will reach us. (422)

This is where Elizabeth's story comes in. In 1979, Elizabeth wants to find out more about the war, but everyone has forgotten. She asks her friends and colleagues what they know about it and is met with indifference, "I don't know when the wretched thing was," one of them answers, before referring to it as "ancient history" (256); "I don't think about the war", another says (257). Elizabeth concurs: she was taught about it at school, but "I don't seem to have been paying much attention. It all seemed so boring and depressing, all those battles and guns and things" (257).

Elizabeth represents an England that has become, in the words of the great poet, Geoffrey Hill, "a nation/with so many memorials but no memory".* Faulks wants to address this – he wants to make us remember, to make the past become a vital aspect of our present. We could not live the lives we do, he wants the reader to feel, without this war. "People don't always appreciate the sacrifices that were made for them," Elizabeth thinks (393). Faulks wants us not just to appreciate these sacrifices, but to feel them as a constitutive part of our lives. As Nigel Watts wrote in Time Out, after reading *Birdsong*, "one's life is set in a changed context".

One way in which Faulks tries to achieve this is his loving recreation of the textures of everyday life. The war chapters are exciting and dramatic, but Faulks hasn't forgotten that, in between the bouts of fighting, war is banal, that the soldiers in the trenches had a repetitive and boring daily existence. As such, there are long stretches of the novel in which nothing happens. Faulks is known for his brilliant use of detail to bring a scene vividly to life, something we can see in his descriptions of life in the trenches. He writes, for example, about how the tea the soldiers drank tasted "of petrol, from the cans in which it was carried" (360); about how it feels to wear uniforms with "lice along the seams" (137); about how the soldiers got to know

Birdsong is richly concerned with the inadequacy of memorial, of erecting "only granite slabs in place of living flesh, on whose inhuman surface the moss and lichen would cast their crawling green indifference" (236).

the "contours" of each others bodies because they were forced to sleep so close together (297). Every page is bursting with details like these, and as George Garat wrote in the LA Times: "The sensuous, affective surfaces, the details, the fully imagined physicality of life and death are so powerful as to be almost unbearable."

This exacting attention to detail is a key reason for the novel's success, says the critic John Mullan. Some readers have complained of Stephen's "coldness", but this is to miss the point. "His emotions cauterised and his memories almost cancelled, Stephen becomes a sensory instrument." There is almost no anger about the horrors he witnesses (it's left to the reader to feel angry), but there is plenty of disgust.

Through him we get the smells and the slime, the rats and the lice. "Nothing he had foreseen, nothing he had dreamed of could have bodied forth the shape and taste of this existence." And it is "shape and taste", rather than moral attention, that fill his thoughts.

This use of realistic details allows Faulks to draw connections between the three periods. Look at the motif of clothing, for example. Clothing has special significance in *Birdsong*: Stephen works in the textile industry; his granddaughter runs a high-street fashion brand. Elizabeth's business – a mass manufacturer of cheap clothing – would not be possible without the machines that put the workers out of work in Amiens in 1910. Similarly, it was factories like Azaire's that made the soldiers' lice-infested uniforms (in the BBC adaptation this is made more explicit: we actually see his workers making the uniforms). Stephen is always attentive to the "peculiarities" of men's clothing, says Mullan: "the different kinds of stench of different fabrics, the exact materials with which the soldiers line their boots". With his emphasis on the reality of the clothing industry, Faulks makes us aware of the complex chains of human endeavor that lie behind the seemingly inconsequential details of everyday life. So we see how interconnected the different time periods are. But when we compare the soldiers' lice-infested uniforms to Isabelle's elaborate and fashionable costumes, and the cheaply produced garments that Elizabeth sells, we can also see just how different they are.

The same is true of the subterranean tunnels that connect the periods: when we are first introduced to Elizabeth, she is in "the tunnels of the Underground" (243). Immediately, we remember the men digging under no man's land. But Faulks makes the link more specific: Jack Firebrace got his job as a tunneler in the war because he was part of the team which dug the Central Line: the very line Elizabeth is on. Even the language Faulks uses to describe her train chains it to the war: it "fitted its tube like a bullet in the barrel of a rifle" (251). But while the tunnellers experienced extreme claustrophobia, what Elizabeth feels is "impatience". Once again, Faulks is using the details of everyday life to draw connections between the time periods, while also showing just how different they are. Life in London in 1978 is very different to life in the trenches in 1916, yet what happens in 1978 would be impossible without what happened in 1916: Elizabeth would not be sitting on a Central Line train were it not for Jack Firebrace.

We don't just see the past in the present in *Birdsong*; we see the future in the past, too. When, Stephen goes on what should be a pleasant boat ride on the backwaters of the river Somme, he sees death and decay, a premonition of the war:

> *The brown waters were murky and shot through with the scurrying of rats from the banks where the earth had been dug out of trenches and held back by elaborate wooden boarding... What was held to be a place of natural beauty was a stagnation of living tissue which could not be saved from decay. (44)*

The "brown water", the "rats", the "trenches", the "wooden boarding": this is what his daily life, four years later, will consist of (and see how expertly that phrase "shot through" is placed; six years later, it will have a very different significance). Later, Stephen visits a church in Amiens and experiences another premonition, "a picture in his mind of a terrible piling up of the dead" (71). Again, six years later, this surreal image will be his reality.

The effect of this emphasis on the continuities and contrasts of everyday life is a kind of defamiliarisation: when, in the build-up of detail, we experience the everyday life of the man who dug our tube tunnels for us, learn about the extremity of his suffering and compare that to Elizabeth's indifferent boredom, a ride on the London Underground becomes a very different experience. Faulks wants us to become aware of the human effort and suffering that has led to our easy and comfortable lives, to remember and to be thankful.

Love

Red, the colour of blood, is the predominant colour in *Birdsong* . There's Isabelle's "blood-red skirt" (12); the "red room" that she and Stephen first make love in (58)*; the "red ribbon" a prostitute wears in her hair, and the "red lamp" that lights her room (204); Elizabeth's earrings are "the colour of oxblood" (251), and when she eats at a restaurant after visiting the battlefields, she sits on a "red plastic-covered bench" and watches "as the juice

*There's a "red room" elsewhere in English literature. Jane Eyre is locked in one; many psychoanalytic critics have compared it to the womb.

from [her meat] furred the edges of the potatoes, turning them red" (262). And then there are all the wounds and bleeding in the war, set against "the pink swell of divided flesh" between Isabelle's legs and her menstrual bleeding (60). One of the war veterans in *Regeneration* says of the colour red: "whatever it is, even if it's a flower or a book – it's always blood". The same is true of *Birdsong*: every page of the book is blood-spattered and blood impels everything. We know Isabelle desires Stephen because of the "blood rushing into her face" (30); we know Stephen desires Isabelle because his "flesh was rigid and swollen with blood" (73). We know the war is a catastrophe because of the blood spilt on the earth. *Birdsong* is unflinchingly bloody and unflinchingly bodily.

The famously erotic first part of the novel is especially graphic. Just look at this passage:

his tongue, lambent, hot, flickering over and inside her, turning like a key in the split lock of her flesh. This shocking, new sensation made her start to sigh and shudder in long rhythmic movements, borne completely away on her passion, feeling a knot of pressure rising in her chest, a sensation that was impossible to sustain, to bear, though all its momentum seemed to be onwards. In this conflict she thrashed her head from side to side on the bed. (59)

This is a description of a body pushed to its limits, and has much in common with Faulks's writing about war: the emphasis on forward motion ("all its momentum seemed to be onwards"), on new extremes ("this shocking, new sensation"), on an almost painful physicality ("impossible to sustain, to bear"). And look at the violence of the language: "In this conflict she thrashed her head from side to side." Later on the page, when Stephen enters her, Faulks describes it as an "impalement". This is the language of war describing the experience of love. As Faulks wrote in his introduction, the "flesh-and-blood sequences" in the first 100 pages are "the corollary of the bodily dismemberments" in the war sections.

Birdsong is about what happens to the human body in love and war. Love, as another extreme of human experience, is part of the same world as war: when Stephen, in the trenches, thinks back to his time in Amiens, he thinks: "What had taken place beneath that placid irregular roof seemed to him to belong to a world as peculiar and abnormal as the one in which he now lived" (158). For Faulks, the act of love and the act of war are both extreme events which tear through the fabric of normality, defy comprehension and change things for good. Thus, after Stephen and Isabelle have made love for the first time, Isabelle feels as if she is "at the start of some descent whose end she could not imagine" and asks Stephen: "What have we done?" (61). Michael Weir asks the same question after the Somme: "What have we done? We've done something terrible, we'll never get back to how it was before" (239).

As the novel unfolds sex and war, pleasure and pain, become harder to disentangle. There is a disturbing scene, for example, in which Stephen, having learnt that the 32-year-old Weir has never had sex, takes him to a prostitute in a nearby village. Weir can't go through with the act so Stephen tries to take over. But when he sees the girl lying naked on her bed he can't stop thinking about dead bodies:

> *When he looked at the girl's upper body, the ribs and spine, he thought of the shell casing that stuck from Reeves's abdomen; he thought of the hole in Douglas's shoulder where he had pressed his hand through almost to the lung. (206)*

Her body is "no more than animal matter" and as a result he "did not know whether to take the girl or kill her" (206).

When in 1917 Stephen sees Isabelle for the first time since their affair in 1910, she has suffered an injury and has a facial scar. Their meeting is cold, but when he says goodbye Stephen touches the scar. In Faulks's description of her response, the scar becomes a symbol for the way the bodily experiences of sex and war have become entangled:

She was overcome with desire as his fingers probed
the abrasion. It was as though they were not on her
cheek, but were opening the flesh between her legs;
she felt again the soft intrusion of his tongue; she
re-experienced the ecstasy of abasement and
possession. (336)

But there's more to love than sex. And while most
reviewers spotted the link between sex and death
in the novel, some found it harder to find a
connection between love and war. What, the
novelist Michael Gorra asked in the New York
Times, does this love story have to do with life in
the trenches? The book is about war: why do we
have to read a hundred pages of soppy romance
before we get there? Gorra thought the war
sections of the novel "superb... daily life in the
trenches... has scarcely ever been presented in such
unrelenting and dispassionate detail," but that the
novel "runs into problems" with the love story:
"[Stephen's] affair with Isabelle has little bearing
on the war narrative proper."

Is Gorra right about this? According to the
psychologist William Rivers, in Pat Barker's
Regeneration:

One of the paradoxes of the war – one of the
many – was that this most brutal of conflicts
should set up a relationship between officers and
men that was... domestic. Caring... The war that

had promised so much in the way of "manly" activity had actually delivered "feminine" passivity, and on a scale that their mothers and sisters had scarcely known.

Faulks, surely, is making a similar point, with Isabelle and Stephen's love for each other mirrored by the love that the affection-deprived men in the trenches learn to show to one another. The men became each other's wives, sisters, mothers; the love and affection that they had previously relied on the women in their lives to provide now had to come from other men. Barker explores the latent homo-eroticism in the trenches – and the crisis of masculinity that the war created – to a much greater extent than Faulks does, but there is no doubt that there is a second love story in *Birdsong*: love in the Trenches.

Love and war "always seem to go together in fiction", says John Mullan. "In ancient literature, it is love that makes men fight; in unheroic ages, the relationship is less direct." Faulks's "unromantic" choice is to have his protagonist forget the woman he loves once he is in the trenches. "The novel forgets her too: in its pre-war first section, some passages are narrated from her point of view" but once she and Stephen are separated, "she is gone".

It is rather that the sensual detail of their brief time as lovers is horrifically parodied by Stephen's physical life as a soldier. The love scenes are there to alert you to what the body can feel, and to exhibit Stephen's peculiar sensuality. He notices the veins beneath a woman's skin, the flush of flesh. Later, he will not be able to help noticing exactly what bullets and shells do to flesh all around him.

As Mullan says, for some time Faulks's working title for the novel was *Flesh and Blood*, a phrase that recurs throughout it. Indeed Stephen finds the terrible things done to men's flesh easier to recall than their faces or characters.

> *He recalled individual limbs, severed from their bodies, and the shape of particular wounds; he could picture the sudden intimacy of revealed internal organs, but he could not say to whom the flesh belonged.*

Intimacy is "just the word", says Mullan, for Stephen's knowledge of precisely what bullets and shells do to human bodies. "In many ways, some of them perverse, *Birdsong* is a story of intimacy." First we are shown the passionate, secret intimacy between Stephen and Isabelle, its intensity heightened by the "formality" with which they have to behave towards each other. Then comes Stephen's intimacy with his fellow soldiers. Trapped, finally, in a collapsed tunnel, he and Jack Firebrace both seemed doomed to die, and, says Mullan, "are forced into a desperate intimacy, the closeness of two living corpses".

Sebastian Faulks (b. 1953) was appointed CBE for services to literature in 2002

Earlier, we have been told that Jack Firebrace "depended on the resilience of certain men to nerve himself to his unnatural life," and that "Arthur Shaw, with his handsome, heavy head and calm manner was his greatest inspiration" (142). "Handsome" certainly hints at a latent homoeroticism. And later, after Shaw is killed, Jack is reminded of his feeling of grief when he learnt of his son's death, and thinks: "I have made this mistake in my life... not once but twice I have loved someone more than my heart would bear" (345). More than my heart would bear: this is the language of romance.

Stephen and Weir have a romance, too. When they find themselves in a shellhole together, after the Somme, the short scene between them is

TEN FACTS ABOUT
WORLD WAR ONE

1.

Britain was the only country to fight both World War
One and World War Two on the side of the allies from
the first day to the last.

2.

Both the British King, George V, and the German
Kaiser, Wilhelm 11, were grandsons of Queen Victoria.

3.

The German trenches tended to be less squalid than
the British and French ones. German bunks were
more comfortable and the cooking facilities better.

4.

By the end of the war, more than nine million soldiers
had been killed, another 21 million wounded. More
than a million soldiers were killed at the Somme,
including about 30,000 in just one day.

5.

Around 11 percent of the population of France was
killed or wounded during the war.

6.
The Western Front was very noisy. In 1917, the explosives used to destroy a bridge in France were heard more than 130 miles away in London.

7.
A total of 12 million letters were delivered to the front every week during the war. Astonishingly, it only took two days for a letter from Britain to reach the front. By the end of the war, two billion letters and 114 million parcels had been delivered.

8.
The youngest British soldier, Sidney Lewis, was 12 years old, having lied about his age when he joined up. He was one of thousands of eager underage boys who enlisted. He survived the Somme.

9.
Despite the horrific death toll, nine out of 10 British soldiers survived the trenches.

10.
The idea that incompetent generals sat out the war in comfort is a myth. So many senior officers insisted on going over the top that eventually generals had to be banned from doing so.

as romantically powerful and as tender as any
Titanic or *Twilight*:

> *"Hold me," said Weir. "Please hold me."*
> *He crawled over the soil and laid his head against*
> *Stephen's chest. He said, "Call me by my name."*
> *Stephen wrapped his arm round him and held*
> *him. "It's all right, Michael. It's all right, Michael.*
> *Hold on, don't let go. Hold on, hold on." (240)*

Reading Stephen and Isabelle's story primes us for
these moments: like the men, we feel the absence
of love and look for it in unexpected places.

But the love story has another, more
complicated resonance in *Birdsong*, and to
understand it we need to look closely at the motif
– which spans all three time periods – of
claustrophobia. The war sections are literally
claustrophobic, most memorably in the tunnels,
where there is not even enough oxygen to light a
match: "The match burned bright red but would
not flame" (123). There's a more metaphorical
kind of claustrophobia in the chapters about
Elizabeth: she is hemmed in by triviality. Her life is

> *a rush and slither of trivial crises; of uncertain*
> *cash-flow, small triumphs, occasional sex and too*
> *many cigarettes; of missed deadlines that turned out*
> *not to matter... (414)*

These trivial crises constrict "a larger life inside her... something unfulfilled, something needing to be understood" (254). A striking contrast to Stephen, who is trapped for a number of days under "several hundred thousand tons of France" (12), Elizabeth is buried underneath the banal minutiae of everyday life in 1979.

But it is Isabelle's claustrophobia that reveals the most. The Azaires' household is a world constricted by social custom and propriety, with no room for love. In his introduction, Faulks writes: "I wanted the texture of the prose to increase the sense of social and sexual claustrophobia and to suggest a kind of period formality." And it does. Look at this description of Azaire's attitude to the children he wants Isabelle to bear, for example: "He saw the production of further children as an important proof of his standing in society and a confirmation that this was a balanced match"(38).The language here – "production... proof... standing... society... confirmation... balanced" – allows no room for love in the business of procreation: it is simply a case of proving one's social standing. (The novel's attitude to bearing children is, we'll find, quite different.)

Faulks's language in the opening section is almost too exact, which makes the reader feel the weight of all the unspoken rules and contracts and conventions that governed the social life of the period. Here are Stephen and Isabelle sitting side by side in a boat, trying to avoid touching, the angles of their feet over-exactly described:

> *His polished leather shoes lay on the slatted wooden floor of the craft at the unnatural angle required by his feet if they were not to touch the white shoes of Madame Azaire, which lay together in the position dictated by the slightly sideways attitude of her closed legs. (42)*

Or consider the opening of the novel, which describes the street the Azaires live on: "The town side of the boulevard backed on to substantial gardens which were squared off and apportioned with civic precision to the houses they adjoined." This is a language of portion and containment: "squared off... apportioned... precision". But it is followed by a description of the bottom of the gardens, which

THE GARDENS

The critic Daniel Soar, in the London Review of Books, picked up on the description of the gardens in *Birdsong*, writing about how appropriate the choice of words is: "when you look closer... you find that the Latinate words are very purposefully derived by way of French: *adjoindre* is more common in French than its equivalent is in English; and 'precision', here, carries a meaning that is slightly less obsolete in French than it is in English, that of cutting off or trimming, have a "wild, overgrown look" with "deep lawns and bursting hedges" (3). There is always something uncontainable, something waiting to burst out of the circumscription. In Isabelle's case, the wildness is something inside, a passion, "a larger life inside her", "an accumulation of natural impulse and affection that had not been satisfied by any of the circumstances of her life" (38) which, like the unlit match, has "burned bright red but would not flame" but which Stephen will ignite.

Stephen recognises this quality of wildness in Isabelle immediately, as evidenced by the code-word he uses to describe her in his diary after their first meeting: pulse. Here is the relevant passage, a good example of how skilfully Faulks can build up a life out of tiny, seemingly inconsequential material details (note, too, that blood is once again important):

making the sentence just tautological enough ('squared off', 'apportioned', 'precision') to turn it into a display of how elegant variation can be when you know your stuff."

Indeed, much of this first part of the novel reads rather like a translation from French. When Bérard says, "There it is, there it is" (8), it is as if his French speech – "Voila, voila" – has been translated. Other rather clunky formulations – "As they finished dinner there was a ring at the front door" (7) – sound smoother in French, too – *Comme ils ont fini le dîner il y avait un anneau à la porte d'entrée.* The uncanny feeling of reading a foreign language that has been translated increases the feeling of claustrophobia •

It seemed to him... to suggest something of his suspicion that she was animated by a different kind of rhythm from that which beat in her husband's blood. It also referred to an unusual aspect of her physical presence. No one could have been more proper in their dress and toilet than Madame Azaire. She spent long parts of the day bathing or changing her clothes; she carried a light scent of rose soap or perfume when she brushed past him in the passageways. Her clothes were more fashionable than those of other women in the town yet revealed less. She carried herself modestly when she sat or stood; she slid into chairs with her feet close together so that beneath the folds of her skirts her knees too must have been almost touching. When she rose again it was without any leverage from her hands or arms but with a spontaneous upward movement of grace and propriety. Her white hands seemed barely to touch the cutlery when they ate at the family dinner table and her lips left no trace of their presence on the wine glass...

Yet despite the formality towards him and her punctilious ease of manner, Stephen sensed some other element in what he had termed the pulse of her... perhaps only in the tiny white hairs on the skin of her bare arm or the blood he had seen rise beneath the light freckles of her cheekbones, he felt certain there was some keener physical life than she was actually living in the calm, restrictive rooms of her husband's house with its oval doorhandles of polished china and its neatly hatched parquet floors. (22-23)

The build-up of socially-claustrophobic material detail in the first part of this passage suggests just how constricted Isabelle is. There is always a disjunction between the materials and her self: when she stands up it is with no "leverage from her hands and arms"; when she drinks "her lips left no trace of their presence". Faulks wants us to see just how against her nature is the role she has been forced to adopt, drawing a distinction between the "restricted" physical world she inhabits – "oval doorhandles of polished china and... neatly hatched parquet floors" – and her inner life – "the blood he had seen rise beneath the light freckles".

And once again, we see the importance of clothes in the novel: a dichotomy is established between her clothes and her body. Her clothes constrict her, they hide her real, inner self from view. But in her body Stephen sees a kind of sensuality, an erotic openness, an uncontainable in-tune-ness, which marks her out as special: "the pulse of her, that concealed rhythm of her desire that expressed her strange humanity" (217).

Much later in the novel, after the Somme, when he is on leave and walking through the countryside in north Norfolk, Stephen has an epiphanic moment of communion with the world; he feels a "passionate affinity" for the: "rough field"

running down to the trees and for the path going back into the village where he could see the tower of

the church: these and the forgiving distance of the
sky were not separate, but part of one creation, and
he too, still by any sane judgement a young man, by
the repeated tiny pulsing of the blood, was one with
them... (363)

(Here are those words again: "pulsing of the blood".) This affinity is a "force of binding love" which makes him want to "stretch out his arms and enfold in them the fields, the sky, the elms with their sounding birds" (363). Again, later: "There were no distinct worlds, only one creation, to which he was bound by the beating of his blood" (437). The "beating of his blood" is part of a natural rhythm and his awareness of it makes him realise how bound together are the disparate threads of creation (much like the novel's disparate threads). This is a love that Stephen has learnt from Isabelle: an openness to the rhythms of the world which leads to a release from the constricting forces of life.

This is what saves him from the war. When he is trapped underground at the end of the novel, and thinks he is about to die, Stephen tells Jack the story of his affair with Isabelle. He concludes:

There was something in what happened between us
that made me able to hear other things in the world.
It was as though I went through a door and beyond it
there were sounds and signals from some further
existence. (472)

The memory reminds him of his experience in Norfolk, the feeling of love for the world, and gives him the strength to try to escape:

His thirst and fatigue were forgotten; he was alive with a passion for the world, for the stars and trees, and the people who moved and lived in it. If they could not reach him, he would throw off the walls of the earth, he would scratch, eat and swallow his way out of them and up into the light. (481)

With this new lease of life, he begins tapping on wood – a signal his rescue party hears and uses to find him. And when, on being rescued, he sees that his saviour is one of the enemy, his response is an unexpected gesture of love. He spreads his arms; they hug and weep; the war is over and they are free:

Levi guided Stephen's slow steps up the incline towards the light. They had to cover their eyes against the powerful rays of the sun. Eventually they came up into the air of the German trench... they could hear the sound of birds. The trench was empty. (484)

The movement from constriction to freedom as the result of love is one that the love story and the war story share. And far from being irrelevant, the love story literally saves Stephen.

Birth

Stephen's emergence from under the ground is a kind of rebirth. Every time he emerges from the tunnels it is as if he is being born again:

> *He climbed the shaft of the mine with growing pleasure. Up in the mud, in the yellow light, beneath the rain, he stretched his arms and breathed deeply on the chloride of lime as though it were the finest scent from the rue de Rivoli. (307)*

The tunnels, like the "red room", are womb-like. *Birdsong* is intricately patterned with images that suggest giving birth – a pattern which culminates, of course, in the final chapter, with Elizabeth giving birth to her son. Right from the beginning, the novel is concerned with mothers, with what it means to be – and to have – a mother: Stephen has no mother and Isabelle no children; this is part of what draws them together. Isabelle mothers Stephen: she feels "motherly tenderness" towards him (40); when they first make love she calls him "My poor boy" (58). Later, she "felt proud of him... She wanted to take the credit for him, to show him off and sun herself in the approval he would win" (65). Just like a mother would.

Like Stephen before the war, the soldiers on the Western Front are starved of maternal affection and regularly call out for their mothers at the moments of their most extreme suffering: Stephen when he nearly dies (177), Jack when he realises he will die underground (456). "'They always do,' said the medical officer" (177). "Every one of the men we've killed is someone's son," Stephen tells Jack (136). Later in the novel, when Elizabeth begins to think about her grandfather's generation she finds herself feeling "protective" of them – "she felt almost maternal towards them" (267) – as if even the act of remembering is a kind of motherhood.

The soldiers are just as concerned with their children as they are with their mothers. Most of them see their own fate as sealed; they will either die in battle, in the trenches, or if they live, they will never be free from the shadow of their experiences. As the ever-insightful psychologist William Rivers says in *Regeneration* of his patient David Burns, a soldier: "He had missed his chance of being ordinary." This is why they are so conscious of what comes after them. Thinking of future generations gives them hope. Mothers mean a future: Weir thinks of his mother as "the way the world renewed itself and carried on" (195), and Stephen feels something similar when he visits the prostitute: "she was the possibility of love and future generations" (205). Future generations represent the promise of both remembrance and continuation. When she starts trying to decipher her grandfather's diary, Elizabeth understands this; the war matters to her, because "her own grandfather" fought in it, "her own flesh and blood" (262).

Elizabeth is Stephen's continuation – his release from the horrors of the war. She represents something else, too: she represents us. When she first starts to think about the war, she tries to read a history book about it. But it is not easy:

She found it hard going. It seemed addressed to insiders, people who already knew all the terminology and all about the different regiments... Still, in some of the book's more matter-of-fact moments, the calmly given statistics and geography, there was something that held her attention. Most eloquent of all were the photographs. There was one of a moon-faced boy gazing with shattered patience at the camera. This was his life, his actuality, Elizabeth thought, as real to him as business meetings, love affairs; as real as the banal atmosphere of the cross-channel ferry lounge... his terror and imminent death were as actual and irreversible to him as were to her the drink from the bar, the night in the hotel ahead, and all the other fripperies of peacetime life that made up her casual unstressed existence. (259)

As long as World War One is treated as military history, as a dry series of facts and figures, Faulks suggests, it will have very little place in modern life. But the photographs bring the past alive – they

A scene from the 2010 stage adaptation of Birdsong, *written by Rachel Wagstaff and directed by Trevor Nunn, at the Comedy Theatre in London*

effect a kind of rebirth – and they do so by creating a sense of everyday life, of the war as a lived-through experience. Once Elizabeth sees the photographs, the war stops being a string of "terminology" and becomes continuous with her everyday life, with "the drink from the bar, the night in the hotel", and so on.

Novels do the same thing. With his slow build-up of detail, Faulks recreates the material and psychological textures of everyday life for the men in the trenches; when we read the novel, we live through it with them; we see what they see, hear what they hear, go where they go. History becomes something else: as Elizabeth thinks when she talks to Brennan in his nursing home about Stephen, it "had stopped being history and turned into experience" (210). And so it is with the novel. Both the writing and the reading of it are acts of love that effect a kind of rebirth for the soldiers who died in the war: remembrance as motherhood. As Pat Wheeler has written in *Sebastian Faulks's Birdsong*: "*Birdsong* is Faulks's attempt to 'repopulate the fields' where so many thousands of young men were killed or maimed." Or, if that sounds a little fantastic, it is his attempt to show that they and we are connected: they are a part of us and we are a part of them and like them we will sink into the mud and become a part of the "moist earth" under our feet (124). *Birdsong* is an act of remembrance that, through remembering, expresses love for those who died and, through that, releases them from the fate of being forgotten.

Why is the novel called *Birdsong*?

There's certainly a lot of birdsong in the novel. As with the colour red, if you open the book at any page, you'll probably find a bird singing. Here are a few. After Stephen and Elizabeth first make love:

Neither of them spoke. Both lay quite still. Outside was the sound of birds. (61)

After a particularly harsh assault from the Germans:

In the wonderful quiet when the German guns had stopped, they heard the song of a blackbird. (158)

As they go over the top at the start of the Somme:

Skylarks wheeled and sang high in the cloudless sky. (225)

When Stephen has his moment of communion with nature in Norfolk:

From the tall elms he could see at the end of the field there was a sound of rooks, and a gentler calling of wood pigeons close at hand. (362)

Just before Elizabeth gives birth:

She was glad when the dawn came with a loud, discordant sound of birds. (498)

And finally, the last words of the novel, after Elizabeth has given birth and Robert is exulting:

In the trees above him [was] a roosting crow, which

erupted from the branches with an explosive bang of
its wings, then rose up above him towards the sky, its
harsh, ambiguous call coming back in long, grating
waves towards the earth, to be heard by those still
living. (503)

But why so much birdsong? It has something to do
with the novel's entanglement of war, love and
birth. As we've seen, they are linked by the patterns
of imagery (blood, wombs, mothers) and by
Faulks's descriptions of extreme bodily
experience. Here's Elizabeth giving birth:

In a rush of blood it slithered down into his hands
and let out a single bleat. Its skin was grey and covered
with a whiteish substance, thick and greasy about
the chest and back. He looked down to the angry
purple cord that looped back beneath Elizabeth's
blood-smeared legs, then to the baby's genitals,
swollen with its mother's hormones. He blew into
its face. It cried, a jagged, stuttering cry. (502)

This has the same visceral quality as Faulks's
writing about sex and violent death; it is bathed in
blood and it isn't pretty. But perhaps the most
striking word is the penultimate one: stuttering. It
is hard not to hear the famous first stanza of
Wilfred Owen's World War One poem 'Anthem for
Doomed Youth' here:

> What passing-bells for these who die as cattle?
> Only the monstrous anger of the guns.
> Only the stuttering rifles' rapid rattle
> Can patter out their hasty orisons.

Faulks's entangled language connects Elizabeth's son's birth descriptively to the war. The question Owen is asking is: how will these deaths be commemorated? Only in the "stuttering rifles' rapid rattle", he concludes – i.e. there is no commemoration. Faulks suggests a different answer: not in the stuttering of the mechanical means of death, but in the stuttering birth cry of their descendants.

And there is something else Owen's poem and *Birdsong* have in common. For Owen, the soldiers die "as cattle": they are animals. And notice how animalistic Faulks's description of this birth is. For a start, the baby is "it", not "he". And when it emerges from Elizabeth's "blood-smeared legs" it lets out "a single bleat", like a newborn calf. Elizabeth, too, when she is giving birth, seems, to Robert, an animal:

> *Her wild eyes reminded him of a horse that has finally scented home and clamps his teeth on to the metal bit: no power on earth could stop the combined force of muscle, instinct and willpower as it drove on to its appointed end. (502)*

Human beings are animals, and as such we are part
of nature, and part of the rhythm of nature, a
rhythm of birth and death and rebirth.

At the start of the book, the cycle of death and
decay is seen negatively. On the boat on the canal,
Stephen thinks:

> *All of them... would be taken back by this earth.*
> *Bérard's tongue would decompose into the specks of*
> *friable soil that gardeners rolled between their*
> *fingers... Little Gregoire and Lisette would be the*
> *mud of the banks in which the rats burrowed and*
> *mated. And Madame Azaire, Isabelle... The*
> *tenderest parts of her that his imagination*
> *shamelessly embodied, even these would not outlast*
> *or rise above some forlorn, unspiritual end in the*
> *clinging earth. (45)*

But with the addition of love, the cycle becomes
hopeful: with love there will always be something
to come after, to continue and remember.

Birdsong, in *Birdsong,* always comes before or
after some significant event: sex, battle, birth. It
represents what precedes and what remains. In
itself *Birdsong* is totally indifferent. It is against
this indifference that we can measure humanity
and understand what it means to be human.
Nature, in itself, is indifferent. Love, like war, is a
human affair.

A SHORT CHRONOLOGY

1914 28 July **World War One breaks out**

1916 1 July – 18 November **Battle of the Somme**

1918 11 November **World War One ends**

1953 20 April **Sebastian Faulks born in Berkshire**

1984 *A Trick of the Light,* Faulks's first novel, published

1989 *The Girl at the Lion d'Or*

1993 *Birdsong*

2002 Faulks appointed a Commander of the Order of the British Empire (CBE) for services to literature

2012 Two-part serial based on *Birdsong*, made by the BBC, starring Eddie Redmayne and Clémence Poésy

Sebastian Faulks on
fiction, life and love

———

"I was on many occasions, completely overcome while writing *Birdsong.* I was shaking from head to foot with a mixture of anger and grief, rage and pity. That surprised me; one thinks of compassion as being a fairly downbeat emotion, I had no idea it could be such a raging emotion."

....

"When I first started trying to write fiction in the mid-1970s, I found I just couldn't set a book in England without feeling terribly self-conscious about it. I didn't feel comfortable writing fiction that had all these social pointers in it about whether you lived in Hampstead or Camberwell or whether you ate quiche or chips. All this stuff just bored me to tears and I suppose one of the attractions of France was that it wasn't England."

....

"I am a romantic, in a literary way, by which I mean the Romantic poets, who thought just because a sensation is fleeting doesn't mean it isn't valuable. If the only criterion of value is whether something lasts, then the whole of human life is a waste of time."

....

"If you have only one life, you can't altogether ignore the question: are you enjoying it?"

....

"I've found contemporary Britain difficult to write about because it seems to me to have lacked gravity or grandeur. This is some cultural problem which I don't really understand. It simply isn't the same in the United States."

....

"I believe that love between people is the greatest life-giving force in the world. It's intensely frustrating and inevitably makes a fool of you, but you can't stop going back to it, and it's pretty much the defining experience of a human being."

....

"My ideal relationship with the reader is that at certain points they will have said, 'I'm finding this quite tough, but I'm going to hang in there,' then at the end they will say, 'Oh God, I'm glad I hung on, it was so worth it'."

....

FURTHER READING

Novels by Sebastian Faulks
Faulks, Sebastian, *Birdsong* (1993); *The Girl at the Lion d'Or* (1990); *Charlotte Gray* (London: Vintage, (1999)

Other Novels
Barker, Pat, *The Regeneration Trilogy* (1991, 1993, 1995); *Life Class* (Penguin, 2009); *Toby's Room* (Penguin, 2013)

Cobb, Humphrey, *Paths of Glory* (Penguin, 1935)

Remarque, Erich Maria, *All Quiet on the Western Front* (Propyläen Verlag ,1929)

Films
Attenborough, Richard, *Oh! What a Lovely War* (1969)

Kubrik, Stanley, *Paths of Glory* (1957)

Renoir, Jean, *The Great Illusion* (1937)

Spielberg, Stephen, *Saving Private Ryan* (1998)

Further Reading
Faulks, Sebastian, *Faulks on Fiction* (BBC, 2012)

Fussell, Paul, *The Great War and Modern Memory*

(Oxford University Press, 1975)

Gilbert, Martin, *The First World War: A Complete History* (Holt, 1994)

Graves, Rupert, *Goodbye to All That* (Anchor, 1929)

Hollis, Matthew, *Now All Roads Lead to France* (2012)

Kendal, Tim (ed.), *Poetry of the First World War: An Anthology* (Oxford World Classics, 2014)

Stone, Norman, *World War One: A Short History* (Penguin, 2008)

Internet Links

Gorra, Michael, 'Tunnel Vision', The New York Times (1996)

Faulks, Sebastian, 'How I found the REAL story of *Birdsong* in the mud and blood of Flanders', Daily Mail (2014)

Mullan, John, *'Birdsong* by Sebastian Faulks', The Guardian (2012)

Soar, Daniel, 'Ravish Me', London Review of Books (2009)

Miller, Andrew, 'Interview - Sebastian Faulks', The Independent, 1998

First published in 2015 by
Connell Guides
Artist House
35 Little Russell Street
London WC1A 2HH

10 9 8 7 6 5 4 3 2 1

Picture credits:
p.8 Public Domain image
p.22 Public Domain image
p.28 © Jeremy Sutton-Hibbert/Alamy
p.42 © Geraint Lewis/REX

A CIP catalogue record for this book is available from the British Library.
ISBN 978-1-907776-90-8

Design © Nathan Burton
Written by David Isaacs
Edited by Jolyon Connell

Assistant Editors and typeset by
Paul Woodward and Holly Bruce

www.connellguides.com